Interaction & Web Design Basics
Published in 2012 by Hernán Gonzalez

Please send errors to errata_iwdb@gratier.com

www.gratier.com

ISBN-13: 978-1477507742
ISBN-10: 1477507744

This book was created to provide a basic understanding of the interactive and web design field.

It is intended as an overview for students of design and for anyone who is learning how to design for the Web.

Contents

1. Visual Hierarchy

2. Color Theory

3. Typography

4. Layout

5. Conclusions

Introduction

Creating a high quality website or interactive application involves integrating and applying various principles and theories of design. An understanding of how to make informed selections from the numerous options is key to a seamless creative approach. Familiarity with visual hierarchy, color theory, typography and layout provide a foundation from which to begin. This **Interaction & Web Design Basics** guidebook is an overview of these essential concepts and theories that are utilized to create the best visual experience.

When beginning the design phase of any project, likely the designer has already gathered the required information for the layout. Planning how that information will be conveyed involves an understanding of visual hierarchy. Once the information has been organized into categories, there are a number of approaches to establishing visual hierarchy in a design. Using elements of design such as size, color and weight to present content in a meaningful way, visual hierarchy is essential to produce successful results.

Before undertaking any interactive design project, an awareness of color theory is crucial. Color can evoke powerful emotional responses, therefore this design aspect deserves careful consideration. Color theory is also important for creating harmonious combinations of colors, as specific tools help to produce aesthetically pleasing color schemes. Another major aspect of color theory involves the meaning of colors.

The determinant of whether content is presented in an effective way, typography brings the message of a design into form. Typography involves a variety factors in addition to choosing a legible and readable typeface. With digital content, typography has an expanded range of factors to explore and consider. Some of the particularly important aspects of typography for web design are the color, contrast and size. Typography also involves alignment, spacing, organization and more.

Bringing all of the components of a design together into a unified layout is another major area that requires thoughtful consideration. Therefore thorough research is undertaken to achieve an optimal layout. A layout should help to support the purpose and communicate the goals of a design. The use of visual direction is one effective means of guiding a viewer through the layout visually. Minimalism is an approach that can create aesthetic appeal, helps to feature the most essential content. A balanced layout that is designed based on the principles of unity also promotes interaction in web design.

Visual
Hierarchy

Definition

A visual hierarchy uses elements of design to provide cues about the relative importance of items in a layout. It also helps to direct the flow of attention in a particular sequence, according to the goals of the design. Facilitating the communication and presentation of information, the use of visual hierarchy is essential to web design theory.

Visual hierarchy makes the comprehension of information easier for the viewer, as relationships and meaning are conveyed through visual codes and patterns. This visual information is designed and arranged to support the mind's natural tendency to differentiate, pair and rank objects based on their physical characteristics.

A visual hierarchy is developed by organizing the components of a layout, and assigning priority to items. Based on the categorization and relative significance of items, their visual impact is created. The most important parts of a layout are designed to catch the eye, by creating contrast among the visual aspects.

The main elements of a design or layout that are used to build the visual hierarchy include:

Size – Larger objects take precedence over smaller, as the eye is naturally drawn to the biggest items first. Contrasting sizes help to communicate the essential meaning of a layout. A common example of this is the use of larger fonts for headings, so that the main ideas stand out among blocks of text.

Complexity – Elements of a design that are more detailed tend to rank first in visual hierarchy. For example, an intricate image among a group of simple graphics is more likely to be the focal point that draws the eye.

Color – Contrast within a color scheme helps to categorize, differentiate, and add emphasis to information. For example, a bright yellow area of a design will highlight information in combination with darker or muted colors. Red can be used to add a sense of urgency or importance.

Images – Images or shapes can be used to feature information, as the eye is naturally drawn to images and familiar shapes. An image of a face, as well as circles and triangles have a strong ability to command the attention. Symbols such as arrows can also be used to influence the sequence of perception.

Position – The placement, alignment and orientation of objects influences the visual flow of a layout. Spacing between objects also affects visual hierarchy, as an item that is set apart can have implied importance.

Importance

A hierarchy is an organization of the items in a layout into levels of relative importance. Drawing attention to the most essential items first, a visual hierarchy brings one or more elements of a design into prominence. This helps to bring clarity and organization to a layout, guiding the eye towards the essence of a design.

Using the elements of web design theory, visual weight can be given to the most important aspects of a layout, to capture the eye of a viewer and direct the flow of attention. Also, the relative significance of the supporting aspects in a layout can be distinguished with the use of design.

Communicating the importance of items when designing a visual hierarchy can be accomplished using the basic design elements in a variety of ways. Some examples include:

Scale – When the size of objects are designed in relation to each other, variations can communicate their relative significance. Larger objects command the attention, therefore they are effective at communicating importance. Similarity in size among elements relays the equality of their value. Using a larger font for headings and subheadings to contrast with the body of the text is an example of using scale to signify importance.

LOREM IPSUM
SIT AMET, CONSE
DUIS SOLLICITUDIN
BH IMPERDIET SED. LO

CONSECTETUR ADIPISCING E

UT PULVINAR NIBH IMPERDIET SED

OR SIT AMET, CONSECTETUR ADIPISCING

IN AUCTOR EROS, UT PULVINAR NIBH IMPERDIET SED

LOREM IPSUM DOLOR SIT AMET, CONSECTETUR DUIS SOLLICITUD

Color – The use of bright or bold colors suggests importance. Red and yellow are particularly used to emphasize or highlight text. High contrast colors bring an item to the forefront of awareness. For example, in the image below, a bright colored font in contrast to a dark background and dark colored text stands out:

Lorem ipsum dolor sit amet, consectetur adipiscing elit. Duis sollicitudin auctor eros, ut pulvinar nibh imperdiet sed. Lorem ipsum dolor sit amet, consectetur adipiscing elit. Duis sollicitudin auctor eros, ut pulvinar nibh imperdiet sed. Lorem ipsum dolor sit amet, consectetur adipiscing elit.

Position – An object that is set far apart with the use of white space is more noticeable, so it can be an indication of importance. When an item is aligned in a unique way, importance can be implied. Significance can also be given to components of a design that are at the top and in the center of the layout.

Weight – Bold fonts are used to provide emphasis to phrases, keywords or important concepts. Heavier weighted lines or symbols can also be used to feature the essential aspects of a layout.

Helvetica Neue 95 Black

Helvetica Neue 85 Heavy

Helvetica Neue 75 Bold

Helvetica Neue 65 Medium

Helvetica Neue 55 Roman

Helvetica Neue 45 Light

Helvetica Neue 35 Thin

Helvetica Neue 25 Ultra Light

Repetition – Repeating aspects of a design can represent importance.

Complexity – A layout can be created to make one item stand out, by designing that item in a more visually complex way.

Expressing Meaning

Every aspect of a design makes an impact that contributes to the overall meaning of a layout. Similarities and differences among objects are categorized and arranged in a visual hierarchy, in order to support the message. The visual relationships between the main concept and supporting elements contribute to the meaning of the design.

Ascribing order and meaning, visual contrast helps to express the essence of a layout. As the items in a layout are designed with visual distinctions, the purpose of the design is able to take focus. Bringing order to information involves grouping.

Grouping elements of a design to create meaning can be accomplished by using a combination of the following concepts:

Similarity – The use of congruent sizes, shapes, textures and colors is a common and effective way to denote that items are related or share certain qualities. Consistency in the use of these patterns helps to create familiarity and understanding, as a viewer will recognize the visual characteristics of different types of objects.

Proximity – Aspects of a design that are positioned closely together tend to give the impression of association in function. Items that are placed far apart will be viewed as having a distinct meaning or purpose.

Continuity – When items follow each other in a sequence, they develop a rhythm or pattern that links them together. This is also effective for creating motion and direction, which can direct the progression of meaning in a design.

Similarity   Proximity   Continuity

Alignment – Relationships between items can be inferred based on how they are aligned with one another. A visible or invisible line can define the direction of a design. Balanced proportions and symmetry among objects can also show their relationships.

Closure – Connectedness between items can be implied by the observer with familiar shapes that are worked into aspects of a design. Also, with enclosure, items surrounded by a border or frame are considered to be related.

As a design is tied together using multiple approaches, the effectiveness of communication is enhanced. A more coherent message is communicated with a design that reflects visual order, enabling an observer to understand the meaning of a layout or design more quickly. It also helps to ensure that the essential goal of the overall layout will not be overlooked or misinterpreted.

Visual Complexity

Visual complexity influences the visual hierarchy of a layout, as intricate or detailed items in a design will usually catch the eye before more basic items. However working with visual complexity involves striking a delicate balance, in order to avoid the tense feeling that can result from a design that is too cluttered. Visual complexity can be an advantage or a disadvantage, depending on how it is used and what the purpose of a design or layout is.

Factors that influence visual complexity:

Variety – If there are many different shapes, textures, styles and colors in a design or layout, it becomes more visually involved. The use of too many competing textures and colors can make a design visually overwhelming and loud however. Items that are more detailed are usually more eye-catching than a simple outline of an image.

Quantity – A large quantity of elements within a design makes it appear more complex. However when there are too many items competing for attention, visual complexity can work against the effectiveness of a design. With a smaller number of design elements, it is also easier to notice the important focal points.

Density – A layout that does not have space between objects can appear either very elaborate, or overly complicated. Density can either draw the eye in curiosity, or overwhelm the mind in clutter. Alternatively, the use of white or negative space is often used to create a more relaxed visual impression.

Placement – When design elements are randomly arranged, the layout appears more complex to the eye. Objects that are aligned make a design appear more ordered and simpler. Also, repeating or symmetric placement in a layout reduces the level of visual complexity.

Familiarity – Visual complexity and interest can increased by objects that are difficult to identify within a design or layout. However the mind also tends to be drawn to forms that are more recognizable. Therefore the factor of familiarity can greatly influence visual hierarchy in both ways.

Range – If a design has an expansive range, it will appear to be more complex. Alternatively, when the range of elements or objects in a layout is narrow, visual processing is faster and easier.

Images

Often the most dominant aspect of a visual hierarchy, an image can determine the overall feeling and impression of a layout. Usually images can tell a story or convey emotion faster than words, therefore they are often used to create a first impression.

Images can be literal, symbolic or abstract. A literal image, such as a photograph, draws attention and can usually be easily understood by a viewer. A symbolic image can also be used to create recognition and simply communicate an idea. Abstract images are usually the most complex, and they tend to draw attention through curiosity.

The types of images used within a layout should be selected based on the concept and goal of the design. With a design or layout, contrast among images and other elements helps to create a lively and eye–catching effect.

When creating a design, it is helpful to understand the following components of images:

Point – The basic building block of an image. A collection of points or dots is what ultimately creates a line, shape or pattern.

Line – Created by joining two points, lines of various weights are used to create shape, pattern, texture, space and movement in an image. Vertical, horizontal, diagonal, curvy and contour lines are used to construct images.

Plane – From the basis of a plane, free form and geometric shapes build the foundation of an image. A combination of shapes combine to form images, and shading can be added to make objects appear three-dimensional.

Color – Adds impact and visual interest to a design. Colors within an image can be adjusted with properties such as hue, value and intensity to vary their effect.

Tone – Refers to the degree of lightness or darkness. Tone describes the relationships between colors within a design.

Texture – Visually implied texture enhances and adds dimension to an image. Lines, shapes and patterns can be used to create textures.

Space – Within an image, space refers to the area between objects.

Size and Volume – Size is a relative measurement that can be used to create impact and visual hierarchy within an image. Volume in an image involves the height, width and depth of objects within the design.

Position

The position of objects within a layout is an important aspect of visual hierarchy and web design theory. A well structured design facilitates communication in an aesthetically pleasing way. Positioning can define and express relationships among items, and show their relative importance to the overall layout. Therefore when planning for the positioning of objects, the priority and essential meanings of each item should be considered.

Creating a layout or design with effective positioning involves applying the properties of proximity and alignment. Proximity refers to the amount of spacing around and between objects, images and text in the layout. Alignment describes the positioning of items along a continuous line, and can include a variety of angles and other types of formations.

Proximity

◊   Helps to organize items in a design or layout.

◊   Varying degrees of white space can be used to differentiate aspects of a layout.

◊   Extra space can add emphasis to the most important elements in the design or layout.

◊   Added space or padding increases the visibility of small items.

◊   Spacing between items can guide the attention to create visual direction and rhythm.

◊   Minimal space that is symmetric and equal between objects is effective in indicating relationships or groupings of items in a layout.

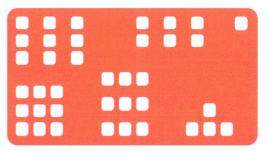

Gestalt Law of proximity

Alignment

◊ Unifies and brings order to the overall look of a design or layout.

◊ Connects and displays relationships among items, as aligned elements tend to be associated with one another.

◊ Angles, lines and shapes can be aligned to create focal points, as the point where two or more lines align or meet will draw the eye.

◊ Visual direction or flow is created when a continuous line is created, whether horizontally, vertically, diagonally or in a shape, curve or some other formation.

◊ Can influence the overall feeling that the design or layout conveys to the viewer, making it either more reserved, neutral or exciting.

◊ Creative alignment that draws the attention can be achieved in a variety of ways, such as with the use of rotational, spiral, or axial alignment.

◊ Spatial progression based on scale and depth is a type of alignment that can be used to show importance of items with size, and spatial progression based on intervals can be used to create visual flow.

Rotational
Alignment

Axial
Alignment

Structural
Focus

Stepping

Spatial Progression:
Interval

Spiraling

Triangulation

Spatial Progression:
Scale/Depth

Color
Theory

The Basics of Color Theory

Color has a dramatic effect, and is often the first aspect of a design that is noticeable to the eye. Color theory is a set of principles used to create harmony among the colors in a design. The way that colors are combined, along with other factors such as saturation and tone, can determine the attractiveness and success of a design. The primary aspects of color theory include the color wheel, properties of colors, harmony and meanings.

The Color Wheel

Representing color theory, the color wheel is a visual representation of the relationships between colors. A tool that can be used for creating color combinations, there are many variations of the color wheel. The most common version of the color wheel is based on the RYB color model, which includes twelve colors.

The color wheel shows the relationships between primary, secondary and tertiary colors:

Primary colors – the three basic colors used to create all other colors.

Secondary colors – created by mixing two primary colors.

Tertiary colors – created by mixing a primary and secondary color.

Primary Colors

Secondary Colors

Tertiary Colors

The color wheel can also be divided into warm and cool colors, which have the following qualities:

Warm Colors – red, orange, yellow, and variations of these colors.

◊ Tend to advance to the foreground.

◊ Often used to create an energetic feel.

Cool Colors – blue, green, purple, and variations of these colors.

◊ Tend to recede into the background.

◊ More subdued than warm colors, creating a calmer feel.

Popularly used in web design, neutral colors such as black, white, gray, cream, brown and beige are not included on the color wheel. These colors are often used to balance or accent a design. Neutrals are also used to create variations in the properties of colors.

Properties of Color

Hue – Defines pure color, mixtures of two pure colors, and can also refer to the set of pure colors within a color space.

Tint – Adjusted by adding white to make a color lighter.

Shade – Created by adding black to make a color darker.

Tone – Involves mixing a pure color with a neutral color, to make a color appear softer.

Saturation – Defines a range from pure color to gray at a constant lightness level; impacts dullness (unsaturated) or vividness (saturated).

Color Harmonies

When creating a design layout, it is important to ensure that the combinations of colors used will be appealing and attractive. Selecting a harmonious color scheme for a design also helps to create visual unity. Harmonious color schemes can be created with a variety of approaches, using the color wheel and the properties of color. Based on color theory, harmonious color schemes consist of two or more colors with a fixed relation on the color wheel.

Following is a summary of a variety of color schemes:

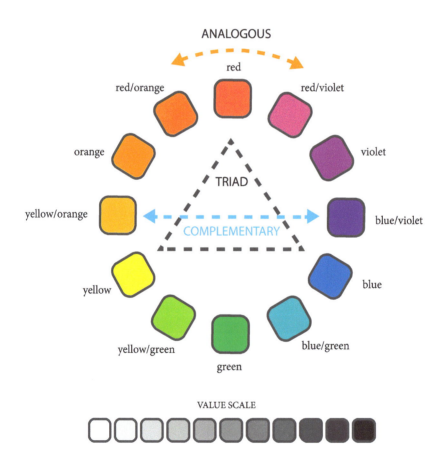

Monochromatic Color Scheme

◊ The simplest color scheme, made up of different tones, shades and tints within a specific hue.

◊ Uses variations in lightness and saturation of a single color.

◊ Is effective at creating a calming, clean or elegant look with a simple appeal.

Complementary Color Scheme

◊ A basic color scheme that consists of two colors that are opposite each other on the color wheel, such as red and green, orange and blue, and yellow and violet.

◊ Variations in tint, tone and shade of the two colors creates more visual appeal and depth.

◊ Works best when a warm color is placed against a cool color, to create high–contrast.

Analogous Color Scheme

◊ Uses three adjacent colors on the 12–spoke color wheel.

◊ Includes one dominant color, one supporting color, and one accent color.

◊ Using different tones, shades and tints helps to create dimension and contrast.

◊ This type of color scheme is usually visually appealing, as it often contains color combinations that naturally occur in nature.

Triadic Color Scheme

◊   A diverse color scheme that uses three colors that are spaced
    equally around the 12–spoke color wheel.

◊   Creates vibrant, harmonious, balanced and rich color schemes.

◊   Has a lower level of contrast than the complementary scheme, but
    still provides strong visual contrast.

◊   Requires that the selected colors are carefully balanced, in order to
    avoid loudness or overstimulation.

Split–Complementary Color Scheme

◊   A variation of the standard complementary color scheme, uses a
    base color with two colors that are adjacent to its complement.

◊   Creates an equally high level of visual contrast as with the
    complementary color scheme, however does not create as much
    tension.

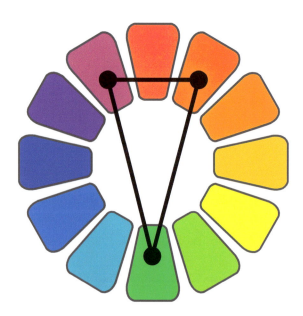

Additional Color Harmonies

Square Color Scheme

◊ Includes the four colors spaced evenly on the color circle, connecting to create a square shape.

◊ Requires achieving the right balance between warm and cool colors.

◊ Most effective with just one color dominating.

Rectangle (tetradic) Color Scheme

◊ Uses four colors of the color wheel arranged into two complementary pairs, can also be called the double complementary color scheme.

◊ Creates rich color schemes that are great for variations of color.

◊ Can be difficult to harmonize unless the hues are varied in saturation, and a balance is achieved between warm and cool colors.

◊ Works best if one color is more dominant while the others are muted.

Warm Color Scheme

◊ Uses red, orange and yellow to create the energetic and passionate effects of warm colors.

Cool Color Scheme

◊ Uses green, blue and purple to create a more relaxed or subdued effect.

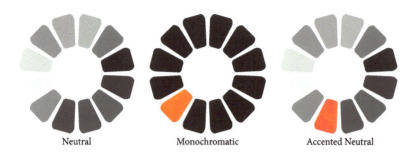

Neutral   Monochromatic   Accented Neutral

Analogous   Split-Analogous   Complementary   Split-Complementary

Triadic   Warm   Tetradic   Cool

Other Important Aspects of Creating a Color Scheme:

Using Neutral Colors

Neutral colors can be used to complement almost any color scheme. Neutrals can make the color scheme of a design feel warmer. Gray will take on a warm or cool feel, depending on the colors that it is paired with. Black and white can also add either a warm or cool touch, depending on the overall color scheme.

Color Dimensions

When creating a color scheme, variations of colors are used to add depth and dimension to a design. The more vibrant colors will appear closer to the viewer, while the more muted colors recede. This can create visual layers that will add interest to the design, making it more lively and dramatic. The four types of variations that can be used include:

Hues – The purest and brightest colors, can be used to create a bold and cheerful appeal.

Tints – Paler colors that can have a calming effect, also called pastels; these colors have white added.

Shades – Often used as accents, these deeper colors are made by adding black to a color.

Tones – Can be used to create a sophisticated or subdued feel, by adding both white and black to a color.

Hue

Tint   Shade   Tone

Color Meanings

Colors can communicate meaning in a variety of ways. Different colors can be used to influence mood, encourage action, and create physiological responses. Color can have a strong impact on the feeling of a design. Colors can also have conflicting meanings that are determined by their context. For example, some shades of blue can evoke a feeling of sadness, while other shades have an energetic or electric quality.

It is especially important to remember that differences in the interpretation of colors are found throughout the world, as cultural influences can create completely opposite reactions to colors from one country to the next.

Following is a summary of the meanings, symbolism and feelings that colors can evoke.

Warm Colors

Red

Red is an intense and captivating color, with a hot, fiery and passionate feel. It is a powerful accent color, often used to denote importance. Useful in communicating danger warnings, red can also be used to symbolize both anger and love. Red can evoke a physical response, therefore it is usually used sparingly in designs.

Orange

Perceived as more inviting and welcoming than red, orange is useful for drawing attention without being as overwhelming. Orange has an energetic quality, and can create a feeling of change and movement.

Yellow

As the color of the sun, yellow is usually seen as the brightest color. Therefore yellow is ideal for highlighting text or elements of a design. Yellow has been used for various causes to represent hope. It is also used to warn of danger, however usually less effectively than red.

Cool Colors

Green
Green is an earthy color with a natural feel, and is often used for environmental causes and organizations. Green can be used to convey a refreshing, healing quality. Often used to create a harmonious feel, green can also represent envy or jealousy.

Blue
Blue is a popular color that is usually well received. A favorite color of many people, it is commonly used in business. Blue has a variety of positive associations, including stability, loyalty and integrity. Blue is typically considered to be a masculine color.

Purple
Also referred to as violet, purple is considered to be the warmest of the cool colors. Purple can evoke a sense of imagination, inspiration and creativity. It is frequently interpreted as a dynamic and active color. Purple can also be used to convey a sense of sophistication and elegance.

Neutral Colors

Black
Black is commonly associated with power, elegance, sophistication, tradition and formality. It can have a range of effects from conservative and sophisticated to modern and edgy, depending on the color scheme.

White
The opposite of black, white creates a neutral background that draws colors out. White can symbolize purity, goodness and virtue. It is also often associated with healing and innocence. White is effective for conveying a feeling of cleanliness, simplicity and minimalism.

Ivory
Ivory is a muted variation of white, which can be used to obtain the benefits of white, while reducing the starkness of contrast.

Gray
Gray can convey formality, sophistication and professionalism. It is often used to create a conservative appeal, while conveying reliability, security and balance. Gray often has a cooling effect, however can be warm depending on the color scheme.

Brown

Brown is a natural, earthy color that is often associated with wood or stone. Often interpreted as a comforting color, brown can communicate simplicity, dependability and reliability. Brown has a warm feel, however it is sometimes seen as dull.

Beige

Beige is considered to be a subdued, relaxing and comforting color. Depending on the color scheme however, beige can sometimes be perceived as dull. Beige has the warm feeling that brown does, however lighter shades have a cooler feel.

Cream

Cream can have a sophisticated, elegant and calming effect. It tends to have an earthy quality when combined with other natural colors. Cream is considered to be a mix of warm and cool, and is perceived differently depending on the temperature of the color scheme that it is used with.

Typography

Typography

Typography
Since Digitalization

Involving the creation and arrangement of text across a wide range of mediums, typography has evolved over time. Spurring tremendous expansion on the field of typography, the digital age helped to make the art form more accessible, yet also much more involved. Computers and other devices presented the need for many new aspects of typography to be developed. Therefore digital typography was created to address these needs.

In order to meet the demands of the Internet and an increasing assortment of digital media devices and formats, the process of designing of typefaces expanded from the use of uniform typefaces, to non–uniform type. This new approach was needed in order to ensure the legibility and appearance of type on a screen, as opposed to only in print.

Non–uniform type changed the process of designing typefaces. Non–uniform type allows for adjustments to various characteristics, to enable translation into differing sizes and resolutions. Digitally, the appearance of a typeface can change with size, altering the contrast, width, spacing and weight. At each size, characters need to be adjusted for resolution.

Slight variations in characters can also be a result of the process of digitalization. Therefore digitizing involves making sure characters are adequately and evenly shaped. The uniformity of serifs also needs to be ensured, as variations can occur. In addition, the stems of each character must be checked, to ensure that they have the same width.

Another aspect of digital fonts that differs from the traditional print media is spacing. The majority of digital fonts are proportionally spaced, rather than monospaced. This means that fixed spaces must be defined with tabs, as the fonts will not align with word spaces. Also, leading is generally larger with digital media than it is in print. This promotes readability and reduces strain on the eye.

The changes that have occurred in typography since digitalization have allowed for ideas to take expression with greater clarity and precision than ever before. Enhancing and supporting the message of the content, typography creates the essential visual form of ideas. Communicating identity and influencing the overall impression and feel of a layout, the importance of typography can not be emphasized enough.

Legibility vs Readability

Legibility and readability both have a strong impact on the effectiveness of a layout. However understanding the difference between these terms helps to pinpoint the best approach to optimizing the visual impact of a design.

Legibility describes the ease with which individual characters or glyphs can be recognized and identified. Readability refers to how easily and quickly sentences, paragraphs, or other blocks of text can be read. The difference is in reading and processing individual characters, as opposed to the overall flow of a piece.

A variety of factors influence legibility and readability, and some of these aspects can impact both. These factors are summarized below.

Factors that influence legibility:

Point Size – A crucial factor, the use of standard point sizes from 10 to 12 points is considered to be the best range for ensuring that text is legible.

X–Height – Highly legible fonts tend to have a larger x–height (also known as corpus size). The x–height of a typeface is the distance between the baseline and the mean line, most often determined based on the lowercase letter x.

Serifs – Generally considered highly readable in print media, serif fonts have structural details which can make characters more easily distinguishable. However sans serif fonts are more widely used in digital media, as low screen resolutions make serifs more challenging to read.

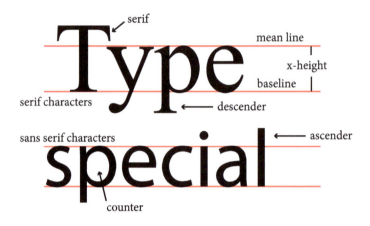

Shape – Simpler, less complex characters are more legible that highly ornate styles, particularly with smaller sized text. Intricate geometric fonts should be reserved for headlines, titles, logos and other short lines of text.

Leading – Very narrow characters are often illegible, while the widest characters usually have greater legibility.

Stroke Contrast – Legibility can be compromised in large blocks of text when there are sharp variations of stroke widths within a character. Bodoni is one example of a typeface with these sharp variations.

Weight – The thickness or weight of strokes within a font can influence legibility. Adding weight makes a font darker, which can alter the shape of a character and reduce legibility. A font weight that is too light may not provide enough contrast with the background to be clearly legible.

Lorem ipsum dolor sit amet, consectetur adipiscing elit. Duis sollicitudin auctor eros, ut pulvinar nibh imperdiet sed.

Times New Roman Regular

Lorem ipsum dolor sit amet, consectetur adipiscing elit. Duis sollicitudin auctor eros, ut pulvinar nibh imperdiet sed.

Times New Roman Bold

Lorem ipsum dolor sit amet, consectetur adipiscing elit. Duis sollicitudin auctor eros, ut pulvinar nibh imperdiet sed.

Times New Roman Italic

Letter Spacing – Inadequate space between letters can make type very difficult to read. Too much space can also impede visual processing.

Legibility vs Readability
Part 2

Organization – Sorting and arranging the content of a layout in a logical way promotes readability. Using the principle of proximity, headings that are placed above sections of text help a reader to more easily progress through the content. Varying type sizes, colors or styles can also help to organize and differentiate content.

Uniformity – A consistent approach using font size, style and color to differentiate and highlight content in a layout improves readability. Consistency in spacing between elements such as text blocks and headlines is also essential.

Type style – A font style with simplicity and horizontal flow supports readability. For blocks of text, cursive, geometric or other embellished text can detract from readability.

Alignment – Has an impact on readability and flow. Text that is justified should be adjusted to avoid awkward or inconsistent spacing between words. Gaps created by white space between words can be adjusted by stretching or shrinking the character, changing the spacing between characters, or by choosing different glyphs.

Line Length – Lines of text that are too long or short can reduce readability. The standard for creating a readable column of text is generally in the range of 45–75 characters.

Effects – The use of effects such as italics, all caps or underlining tends to make text more difficult to read.

Point Size – As with legibility, a point size from 10 to 12 points promotes easy readability.

Color – Finding the right balance of contrast between colors dramatically improves readability.

Leading – Over condensing text creates a crowded feel that can reduce both readability and legibility.

Primary and Secondary Leading – The distance between the baselines of successive lines of type makes text more readable, helping the eye to focus on each line.

Kerning – Adjusting the spacing between characters in a proportional font can help to increase the ease of momentum and flow.

Tracking – The uniform adjustment of spacing over a range of characters can promote readability by improving alignment and character recognition of certain typefaces.

Tracking:

VAULT. V A U L T .

Kerning:

VAULT. VAULT.

Contrast, Color and Size

The use of contrast gives text layouts a dynamic quality, adding to the aesthetic appeal and improving readability. Typographic contrast differentiates elements of the layout, adding visual interest and hierarchy. Contrast can be achieved in a variety of ways, and a combination of approaches is often used. Most commonly, the characteristics of size and color are adjusted in a variety of ways to create visual contrast.

Some of the main aspects of these approaches to building contrast include:

Color

◊ Color contrast is very effective at creating organization in a text layout. Particularly with the Internet, color contrast is frequently used to distinguish between headings, links, body text, and other elements of a layout.

◊ Can determine the effectiveness of communication in a layout, therefore a background that overpowers the text needs to be avoided.

◊ Reversed out text is a style that involves using a lighter colored text on a dark background. Although this can be effective for creating visual contrast, with the wrong color choices it may detract from readability of large blocks of text.

◊ Bright colors are very effective at highlighting and drawing attention to text. However overuse may cause eye strain. Colors that are too pale can also cause strain, slowing down the flow of reading.

◊ Darker, bolder colored fonts are useful for headlines, while lighter colored font weights can be used to minimize the impact of text.

The image below illustrates some of the differences described with regard to color contrast.

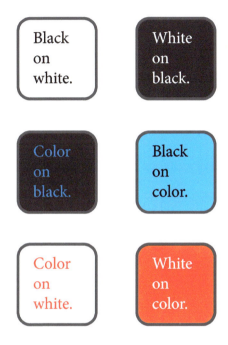

Size

◊   Varying type size is very effective for differentiating content. For example, headlines or titles that have a larger font size than the body text help to create visual contrast.

◊   Image captions, labels and lower priority text can be set at a slightly smaller size than the body text to create visual contrast.

◊   Changing text case is an alternative to size changes for creating contrast. For example, small caps can be used to draw attention to a headline, as the wider characters give the type a distinctive look. However large blocks of text in small caps or all caps can be difficult to read, so should be used very sparingly.

◊   Consistency of application is essential for maintaining balance and organization when using varied sizes of texts.

Layout

Layout

Research

In order to create the most effective end result, the process of building a layout should begin with solid research. When designing a layout, there are many decisions that need to be made that can make or break the success of the design. Research can play a significant role in determining the final outcome, as informed choices will contribute to the likelihood of positive results.

When design decisions are made based on an in-depth understanding of the needs of users, the probability of goals being accomplished increases. Understanding the perspective of the viewer or target audience can open up pathways to increasing functionality, interactivity, and the impact of aesthetics.

Although creating a layout that has a timeless appeal is the goal of many designs, current trends and preferences can be a driving force in the success of some projects. In addition to user research, competitive research allows a designer to embark on the design process with a broader vision of the possibilities.

Gathering the required information takes place through the research process, which can include various phases and methods, such as:

Exploration – Exploring the goals of the design, and identifying the basic questions that need to be answered is the starting point. This phase can include a variety of approaches, such as literature research, brainstorming, sketching, focus groups, and more. An understanding of the target market and the competition is an essential part of information gathering that should be accomplished in the exploration phase.

Observation – Observation can help a designer to understand how a user will interact with a layout. Viewing reactions to a design can show where weakness and unintended effects may occur.

Testing – After exploration and observation have yielded research data, testing the workability of design prototypes is crucial. Ensuring usability and functionality is an important part of this phase. Thorough testing helps to determine whether the aspects of a design will fulfill their objective.

Evaluation - A critical analysis of the data obtained during the testing process is necessary, in order to address any weaknesses or errors in the layout.

Refinement - Improvements and modifications to a layout can be formulated and implemented during the refinement process.

After these phases of research have completed, often a project will be put back through the cycle again, until the final layout has been fully perfected.

Visual Direction

Visual direction that is built into a layout is effective in directing the flow of attention towards a goal. As discussed in the section on visual hierarchy, visual direction can be created to support the message, by contrasting elements of the design in a variety of ways. However when designing a layout with little visual contrast among elements, placing content in specific patterns can help to create visual direction.

Layout patterns are designed to provide a framework for placing elements. These patterns take into account the direction and sequence that the eye naturally follows when reading or scanning content. Using the patterns as a guide, featured elements of a layout are strategically placed to increase their impact.

The following patterns are effective at creating visual direction when a design does not have hierarchy built into other elements such as color, size and images.

The Gutenberg Diagram

◊   Divides a layout into four quadrants.

◊   The top left and the bottom right are the primary focal
     points of the layout.

◊   The top right and the bottom left tend to draw less
     attention.

◊   Visual flow is from the top left to the bottom right,
     supporting the natural flow.

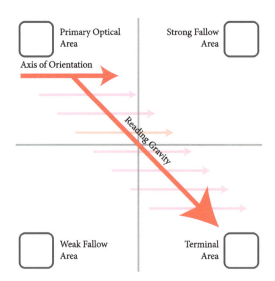

F-Layout

◊   The most important information is featured in the top left, as content placed towards the bottom can be overlooked

◊   Based on studies that show that visual focus tends towards the top left corner and the left side of a layout, with less attention on the right side.

The Z-Layout

◊   Includes four main visual focal points.

◊   Designed in a Z shape, the pattern begins with the natural visual path.

◊   First flows from left to right horizontally.

◊   Second moves diagonally back to the bottom left, and then flows again to the right.

◊   Works well for simpler layouts that do not have many key elements.

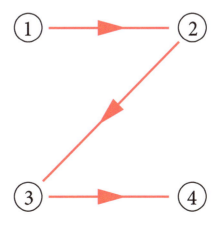

Zig-Zag Pattern

◊ Expands on the z pattern, with a repeating left to right and diagonals.

◊ Effective when there are a greater number of essential elements in the design.

◊ Supports the natural flow of visual direction.

Grid Layout

◊ Items are aligned with a grid that is divided into equal proportions.

◊ Supports the tendency to read from left to right.

◊ An effective way to organize a large amount of content.

◊ Provides structure, and creates rhythm and familiarity.

Minimalism in Design

The approach of minimalism in design is a foundation for the creation of successful and aesthetically pleasing layouts. Minimalistic designs are highly effective at conveying the essential aspects of a layout, while creating a professional, elegant and calming appeal. Minimalistic design helps to narrow the focus to the most important items, which have the greatest weight or highest quality. The 'less is more' approach in minimalism has shown to be very effective, as simpler designs are easier to process and recognize.

Minimalism reduces distractions in a design, so that communication is facilitated. With a minimalistic approach, the quantity of elements that are competing for attention is low. This enables the central message to be relayed and received faster. Also, with less information, the likeliness of all of the items being noticed increases. Using only the most essential elements can also increase the impact or sense of importance that they have. Minimalism can dramatically improve the effectiveness of a design, making interaction and accomplishment of goals easier.

There are a number of features and approaches to creating a minimalistic design, such as:

◊ Narrowing the number of elements in a layout down to only the most crucial content.

◊ The function of objects and elements can be expanded to fulfill more than one purpose, allowing for easier reduction in the number of essential items.

◊ Most minimalistic designs contain a large amount of white space, which provides the contrast to move the attention through the main elements and focal points.

◊ The use of a minimal number of colors, tones and shapes helps to minimize distractions and convey minimalism.

◊ The use of mostly subdued or neutral colors such as white, gray or black, along with only one or two brighter colors helps to promote minimalism.

◊ Designing on a solid color background promotes minimalism, as opposed to a patterned or textured background.

◊ The use of a lower weighted typeface can add to the minimalistic feel of a layout.

◊ Placement of objects along simple lines and angles (such as a grid-based layout) creates more of a sense of minimalism than do uneven or curved edges.

◊ Reducing the size of various items in the layout can help to increase the level of minimalism.

Although all designs do not have to be organized around the concept of minimalism, applying some of these techniques to any layout can help improve the visual appeal and quality of interaction in the design.

Unity

A fundamental principle of design, unity is a visual impression that is created through purposeful creation and order of the visual aspects in a layout. With a unified theme to support the message of a layout, the design as a whole conveys a sense of completeness.

Unity can make a design more accessible and easier to process. As the aspects of a design are tied together in a complementary way, the sense of unity that develops adds to the effectiveness of the layout. The right balance of unity can create a more memorable visual experience. Bringing clarity and focus to the message, unity supports the intention of a layout.

The aesthetic appeal of a design can often be determined based on the visual connectedness of the elements in the layout. Visual harmony can be achieved through unity, as consistency and order contrast with variety to create rhythm.

Aspects of Unity:

Similarity

◊ An essential component of creating unity in a layout or design.

◊ Connections are more easily identified when like items complement each other visually.

◊ The consistent use of color, size, shape, texture, typography, alignment and a variety of other elements can lend to the visual unity.

Color

◊ One of the primary tools for creating unity in a layout or design.

◊ Using an established color scheme with color coding promotes unity.

◊ Helps to portray relationships between elements of a design.

Repetition

◊ Repeating aspects or themes in a design helps to establish unity.

◊ Repetition generates recognition and familiarity.

◊ Enables the processing of information at a faster pace.

Alignment

◊ Connections are interpreted based on the alignment of elements in a design.

◊ Items that are grouped by their alignment contribute to the overall feeling of unity.

◊ A design that is aligned in a balanced way appears more unified.

Proximity

◊ The grouping of items tends to give an immediate impression of unity.

◊ The closeness of objects in a layout can promote a feeling of connection.

◊ Can create interaction between various aspects of a design or layout.

Visual Direction

◊ Elements in a layout are linked together in sequence, as one item leads to the next.

◊ Adds to the meaning of the layout by leading the viewer through the story

Balance

Balance is achieved when the components of a layout create a sense of visual equilibrium. A balanced design usually creates a feeling of harmony, while an unbalanced design can feel chaotic and disorganized. In a balanced design, the visual weights of the elements in a design do not compete with one another. Balance can also largely be determined by the proximity and space between objects in a layout or design.

Proportion is an important aspect of design which can help create to balance. Usually determined by the relative size of objects in a design, proportion is created through the comparative relationship between objects. Many of the greatest designs and works of art use proportion to create visual harmony, which usually makes a design more aesthetically pleasing.

When creating a balanced layout or design, there are several effective approaches including:

Symmetric Balance

◊ Also called 'formal balance,' as symmetry creates an ordered, structured look that creates a sense of formality.

◊ Creates visual unity and repetition.

◊ A symmetric design has a mirror image on both sides when divided by a vertical axis.

◊ Ensures left to right balance.

◊ The center axis is a focal point in a symmetric image.

◊ Designs with approximate or 'near symmetry' contain forms which are equivalent, yet not identical.

◊ With inverted symmetry, often the bottom half of an image is inverted.

◊ Bilateral symmetry is created with both a vertical and a horizontal axis, creating top to bottom balance along with left to right.

◊ Considered to be the most stable form of balance.

Asymmetrical Balance

◊ Also called 'informal balance,' as there is no exact formula for achieving balance with asymmetry.

◊ Can sometimes be considered more dynamic and exciting.

◊ Can be created by balancing a number of smaller items on one side, with a larger one on the other side.

◊ May be used to create visual hierarchy, attracting attention to certain elements.

◊ Designs with asymmetric balance are often divided into thirds instead of halves.

◊ Contrast is created among the various aspects of the design.

Radial Balance

◊ Balance revolves around a central element.

◊ Elements which are equally distributed appear to radiate from a central point in a circular pattern.

◊ This approach makes it easy to create a focal point, as the eye is naturally drawn to the center of the design.

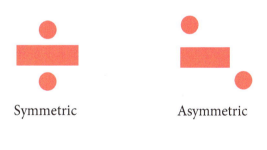

Symmetric   Asymmetric

Radial

Conclusions

Final Conclusions

With a broad range of elements and approaches to web design, an adept designer always continues to refresh and increase their knowledge. Familiarity with the concepts and theories of design expands the range of tools from which a designer can draw from to develop their individual approach to a project.

Using of the principles of design correctly can transform the final outcome of a project. Applying the concepts and theories to a project can often determine whether the result appears amateurish or professional. Effective design principles can also be the deciding factor in whether users understand and identify with the message of a layout enough to interact.

When considering the redesign of an ineffective layout, an analysis of the visual hierarchy, color schemes, typography and layout will usually reveal the areas where there are weaknesses in a design.

A common error in a novice design is the lack of apparent visual hierarchy. A layout that lacks consistency and organization is difficult for users to navigate. This leads to reduced traffic and interaction. Alternatively, clearly differentiated categories and visual relationships support usability and create a more favorable impression.

The use of color also requires understanding and forethought, as it can often create the first impression which can welcome or dissuade users. A distracting, loud or disharmonious color scheme is often a sign that a layout will not be very successful.

Legibility and readability are two more aspects that can often explain the weaknesses of a design. Typography is usually central to achieving the purpose of the layout, therefore it should be developed with insight into the important factors. Improper spacing, alignment, and other factors of typography can impede the interactivity of the design.

The layout of a design also involves a number of factors that need to be applied to ensure that a project fulfills its purpose and function. Insufficient research is often a factor in a design that fails to meet expectations. Lack of visual direction can cause confusion, reducing the effectiveness of a layout. Also, when a balance is achieved between unity and variety, visual interest is maintained rather than lost.

Within each of the concepts and theories discussed in this guide, there are a number of facets that can be further explored for additional examples, ideas and approaches. The world of interaction and web design is an ever expanding field that has revolutionized the creative mediums and potentials.

Notes

www.ingramcontent.com/pod-product-compliance
Lightning Source LLC
Chambersburg PA
CBHW041144050326
40689CB00001B/472